AF240898

WHY THE RICH ARE A PROBLEM

Philippe Richard

WHY THE RICH ARE A PROBLEM

Max Milo

Max Milo, Paris, 2022
www.maxmilo.com
ISBN : 978-2-315-01067-7

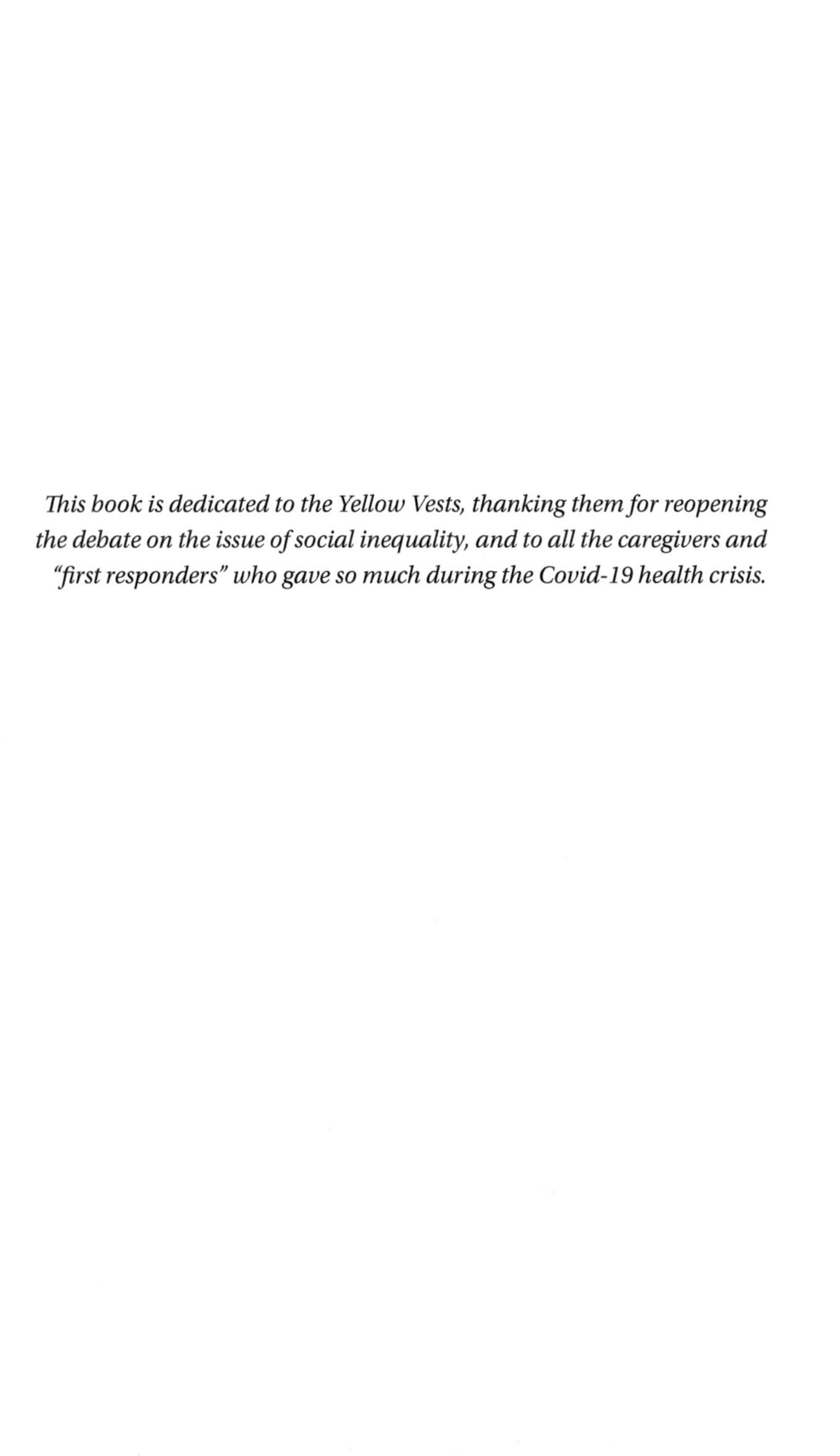

This book is dedicated to the Yellow Vests, thanking them for reopening the debate on the issue of social inequality, and to all the caregivers and "first responders" who gave so much during the Covid-19 health crisis.

Acknowledgements

I warmly thank all the people with whom I could exchange on this thorny issue of the rich, coming from various horizons, from the Copernic foundation, the Attac movement and the Rencontres Déconnomiques, but also from more liberal movements, and a good number of citizens with no marked political affiliation.

This book is a response to all the preconceived ideas I heard about the rich when I published my first book, *Abolir le droit à la fortune,* published by Couleur livres in 2017, and then my second, *Vers une société plus juste : manifeste pour un plafonnement des revenus et du patrimoine,* published by Les liens qui libèrent in 2019 with the Copernic foundation.

Website dedicated to the subject: open-hand.org

Preamble:
Who are the rich?

The objective of this book is to approach without taboo the delicate subject of the rich, through different assertions that we often hear: the rich have always existed because inequalities are natural; by working hard, everyone can become rich; we criticize the rich out of jealousy; the rich consume and invest; bosses create jobs; the rich take risks and innovate; the more rich there are, the less poor there are; the rich pay a lot of taxes...

First, let's start by defining the wealthy class. Who does it include? Is it limited to the 2,000 billionaires on our planet, including a hundred or so in France? Or does it include a vast population that lives comfortably, composed of executives, professionals and small business owners? Neither one nor the other. The rich class is not limited to a few wealthy people, but it is also distinct from the affluent class.

The rich are people with income and wealth that give them economic power in our society. Not only is the wealthy person less dependent on the financial constraints of other social classes, but they also have a great deal of leeway in their economic choices and decisions, the scope of which goes beyond their own circle, impacting a territory, locally or more widely. Thus, his wealth places him in a specific class, quite different from the working class, the middle class and the wealthy, and whose numbers are sufficient to constitute an economic class in its own right.

We now need to determine the wealth threshold that allows access to this class. By considering income and wealth as the two economic reference criteria, we see that these differ from those of the rest of the population for the wealthiest 1% of a geographical area (a city, a region, a country...). In France, for example, the rich earn at least €10,000 net per month and have at least €2 million in assets. These minimums hide great disparities. The average income of the wealthy class reaches €24,000 per month, for an average wealth of €6 million[1]. These amounts explode for some of them.

Classes économiques selon le revenu et le patrimoine - France

Catégorie de population	Part de la population française	Nombre d'adultes	Revenu individuel net mensuel	Patrimoine individuel net de dettes
Extrêmement riches	0,001%	500	> 500 000 €	> 100 000 000 €
Ultra-riches	0,01%	5 000	100 000 € à 500 000 €	30 000 000 € à 100 000 000 €
Très riches	0,1%	50 000	30 000 € à 100 000 €	10 000 000 € à 30 000 000 €
Riches	0,9%	450 000	10 000 € à 30 000 €	2 000 000 € à 10 000 000 €
= Classe des riches	1%	505 500	> 10 000 €	> 2 000 000 €
Classe aisée	9%	4 500 000	3 500 € à 9 000 €	400 000 € à 2 000 000 €
Classe moyenne haute	30%	15 000 000	2 000 € à 3 500 €	135 000 € à 400 000 €
Classe moyenne basse	30%	15 000 000	1 200 € à 2 000 €	10 000 € à 135 000 €
Classe précaire	30%	15 000 000	< 1 200 €	< 10 000 €
Médiane globale		50 000 000	1 500 €	103 000 €
Moyenne globale		50 000 000	1 800 €	215 000 €
Médiane chez les actifs		30 000 000	1 750 €	
Moyenne chez les actifs		30 000 000	2 200 €	

Tableau donné à titre indicatif, à partir des données de T. Piketty, *Pour une révolution fiscale* et réactualisées des rapports de l'Insee et du Crédit suisse. Le revenu est en euros nets perçus avant impôts.

La population regroupe les adultes : les étudiants et personnes au foyer sont rattachés à la classe du référent du ménage.

---

1. Amounts evaluated according to Thomas Piketty's data published in revolution-fiscale.fr and updated according to Credit Suisse Global Wealth Databooks data. These are individualized amounts and not per household.

1. The rich are few,
let's leave them alone

Although the rich represent only 1% of the population, they accumulate a great deal of wealth: more than 10% of the country's income and 25% of all the assets of French households. They share 3,140 billion euros of assets, net of debts. The rich hold 55 times more than the "average" French person. And, unlike the "average" French person who mainly owns his or her main residence (58%), the wealthy own a significant share of the country's businesses and financial investments: 35% of the national economic wealth, excluding real estate[2].

It is therefore surprising that the subject of the rich is so little mentioned in the national debate. Any discussion of the rich is quickly sidestepped to focus on other issues and problems, such as the unemployed, the poor, the delinquents, the migrants, eclipsing any link between the rich and our economic and social difficulties. The premise is simple. The rich are a small, peaceful population, who ask nothing from anyone and actively contribute to the

---

2. Amounts assessed according to data from Thomas Piketty published in Capital et idéologie, Seuil, 2019, from Insee, Le Patrimoine économique national en 2020, October 2021, and French notary statistics on inheritance.

wealth of the country. So let's leave them alone! This is a bit short-sighted, because although the rich are indeed few in number, they nevertheless occupy a central place because of their economic power, the importance of the decisions they make and their consequences. Unlike other social and economic classes, the decisions of the rich impact the whole society. Thanks to their capital, they are the ones who make the decisions to hire, invest, increase salaries, lay off, relocate, increase dividends, expatriate fiscally, etc. Why not talk about it?

A nation certainly needs wealth and capital. Does it really need rich people? Is it a problem that wealth is concentrated in the hands of a minority? The situation can become dangerous for the interests of a nation when a minority holds economic power without protecting the interests of the nation. The rich caste holds more than 35% of the shares of the companies, i.e. the property rights, and therefore the decision-making power. Since they own the big companies, often with significant or even majority stakes, they dominate the whole system, because they are located at the top of the economic pyramid, the one that dictates its conditions and its law.

Finally, France has gone from a monarchy where 1% of nobles reigned, to an oligarchy where 1% of the rich reign. Of course, this reality is not unique to France. While wealth inequality is somewhat lower in Belgium and Japan, it is comparable in the United Kingdom, Italy and Australia, higher in Northern Europe, Spain, Portugal and Canada, and much worse in the United States and in many emerging countries, where the richest one per cent own more than 35 per cent of all national wealth.

The rich make the decisions, and these decisions are not for the greater benefit of the nation as a whole. They have always put their own interests first. The problem today is that the globalization of the economy has been accompanied by deregulations that give freedom to the most mobile. Thanks to the mobility of people, capital and company domiciles, the rich can now escape from their obligations, and they do so without hesitation. The wealthy, their companies and their capital are relocating to tax havens and low-cost countries with impunity. The competitiveness imposed by a globalized economy is in reality only a pretext to conceal the optimization operations of the richest, who do not hesitate to abuse globalization in order to escape national laws and regulations, with the sole aim of making profits.

Economic liberalism has spread throughout the world and benefits the richest, to the detriment of a large majority of the populations of rich countries. The economic development that Western countries experienced during the 20th century seems to be a distant memory. The power of the rich is amplified by their power of influence with the general public, mobilized so that their domination is never questioned. As owners and financiers of numerous media and foundations, they have the power to make and unmake careers, those of politicians, journalists, artists, intellectuals and business executives. In our delegated democracies, which leave little room for the direct participation of citizens, collusion between the rich and elected politicians is the order of the day, since the latter need the support of the former. We then end up with politicians who are particularly attentive to the richest, and who do not question their power, if at all. We often emphasize democracy. Yet it is failing.

Some criticize the migrants who come to take advantage of our country's benefits, the Covid-19 non-vaccinated who do not take their responsibilities towards the nation. Don't the rich take advantage of our country to enrich themselves shamelessly without paying their dues? Do they assume their responsibilities? The rich are few in number but their domination is total. So should we leave the rich alone? No, this impunity must not continue!

2. We criticize the rich out of jealousy

This is the ideal retort to counter any criticism of the rich: it is motivated by jealousy! This easy assertion aims to delegitimize any opposition to this caste with a feeling of guilt, immediately closing any debate. To criticize the rich would be tantamount to not assuming one's own failure, that of not being rich oneself. This is simplistic but effective. This would mean that only the rich have the right to criticize themselves. This is surprising, since many people criticize the unemployed, civil servants and migrants, without being concerned in any way.

Is it a coincidence that the wealth of the ten richest French people has risen from €22.9 billion in 1997 to €240.8 billion in 2017, and then to €516.5 billion in 2021, according to *Challenges*' ranking of France's top fortunes? Ten French people have a fortune comparable to that of half of the French population, i.e. 25 million of the poorest adults. The richest 1% together own as much as 80% of the French population. Is this acceptable and desirable? Does this wealth benefit the country? No.

Here, a fundamental question should challenge us. What is the justification for personal enrichment? If the income from work represents the essential wealth of a country, it is the income from capital that makes the rich. Wealth never comes solely from one's own work, as we shall see, but from the capital one owns, which in turn allows one to draw a rent from the work of others, who precisely have no capital or too little to live on. Thus, according to the Observatory of Multinationals[3], in twenty years, the dividends of CAC 40 companies have increased by 269%, almost four times faster than their turnover (+74%) and ten times faster than their global workforce (+26%). In France, the number of employees has fallen by 12%, while sales have risen by 26%. The owner of a capital asset has the right to the profits and added value of his capital, not the worker, even though it is the latter who enables the capital used to be valorized. It is this right to profit from property that brings personal wealth, not labor.

When you have capital, you can lend, invest or invest it and receive an income from it, even if you have not worked directly to contribute to that income. This is the capital income. And this income can become colossal when the capital is large because it will allow you to benefit from economies of scale, bargaining power and diversified opportunities with high returns. The small saver turns to safer investments with low returns, while the rich person diversifies his investments and ensures high returns. The small trader, the craftsman, the small independent invests all of his capital in a business which, at best, allows him to live correctly, but with limited prospects of gains. The large investor acquires companies or shares in companies with high dividends and growth prospects because he takes advantage of the economies of scale of large companies and their bargaining power and innovation to increase returns. This is called increasing returns. Size thus provides a decisive competitive advantage. This is why companies merge and why multinationals

---

3. "CAC 40: the real annual balance sheet," multinationals.org, November 2020.

prosper, as do billionaires, at the expense of smaller companies. This reality has been reinforced by the development of new technologies in communications that favor the globalization of markets and generate important network effects - an almost infinite source of economies of scale and increasing returns. This is the reason why the founders of the Internet networks got rich so quickly. It was not their work that made their fortune, but the ability of the networks to gather many members, "monetizable" by their owners, with modest marginal costs.

What is important to understand is that wealth is created by human labor and by the use of productive capital that improves labor productivity (machines, premises, patents, etc.). The relevant question then concerns the distribution of the wealth created, between the remuneration of labor and that of productive capital. This is where the problem lies. The share of remuneration of labor has been decreasing for three decades, to the benefit of dividends, the weight of which has globally doubled, and even more so for large companies, generating growing inequalities between on the one hand employees, but also the self-employed and small bosses, and on the other hand the large owners of capital and the multinationals. This is the reason why the working and middle classes in Western countries are becoming poorer. This is a reality, not a feeling (of jealousy).

The criticism of the rich is not based on jealousy but on the perversions of a system that creates a vicious circle, favorable to the richest thanks to the power that capital confers on them, and amplified by an ever more formidable "size" effect, which endlessly reinforces their wealth and domination. Conversely, the situation is getting worse for the less wealthy, as they suffer from the growing bargaining power of the more powerful, demanding ever higher returns, thus imposing price cuts on small suppliers and wage stagnation on workers. More and more of us are caught in a vicious circle: after the unemployed, the precarious and the unqualified employees, come the turn of the small traders and craftsmen, the small bosses, the more qualified employees and civil servants. We can better understand the growing frustrations of the population.

3. The rich have always existed because inequality is natural

This statement is rarely explicit. It often remains veiled, implied. There would be well-born people who deserve wealth, by their talent, their involvement, their know-how - in fact their social origin. History confirms this opinion since inequalities of wealth have often been normalized during the past centuries and in the various human societies.

For all that, can we say that inequalities are natural? Or is it not rather an institutionalization of inequalities, willed and carried out by the dominant, legitimizing their privileges, i.e. their power and their wealth? Is it natural that the highest salaries have seen their share increase by 50% in recent decades in France[4]? Their incomes now exceed 30 times the average income of the French. The French CAC 40 bosses earn a hundred times more than the small bosses, without working more than them. These excesses come to us from the United States, where the incomes of the directors of large American companies have gone from 20 times the average salary in 1965 to 270 times today.

---

4. The weight of the 0.1% of the best paid employees has risen from 2% in the 1950s-1980s to 3% of the total wage bill today, according to INSEE.

The situation is even more favorable for large owners, whose wealth continues to grow, even in times of crisis. One percent of the world's population owns nearly 50 percent of the world's wealth[5]. Thus, 56 million dollar millionaires share $188,000 billion in wealth, net of debt, or 45% of the world's wealth. In ten years, the number of millionaires in the world has doubled and their global wealth has tripled, far from the increase in wealth experienced by the rest of the population during the same period. The wealth of a minority is soaring, as is their income.

Even economic and health crises do not prevent the enrichment of this minority. The money of the central banks flows in abundance to face the crises, mechanically increasing the value of all existing assets, real estate and even more so companies, which benefits the possessing minority. The number of billionaires in the world continues to grow, according to the annual Forbes wealth ranking, rising from 140 in 1987 to 2,720 in May 2021, for a cumulative fortune of 13,400 billion dollars today, compared to less than 300 billion in 1987. Billionaires now own more than three quarters of humanity (the poorest)! Are these 2,720 billionaires worth as much or more than 6 billion people? According to our model, yes. How far will these inequalities go? Will they be sustainable for long?

There is nothing natural about this unequal process. It is institutional, generated by the system in place. Whether by force (dictatorships), by divine right and blood (monarchies and nobility) or by property right (the bourgeoisie), the different systems have always favored the dominant class, because it is the one who shapes them, to its advantage. In our model, it is the bourgeoisie that holds the real power, the economic power derived from the ownership of capital. Of course, beyond economic wealth, the dominant caste has

---

5. Credit Suisse, Global Wealth Databook 2021, June 2021.

always had the means to educate itself, to learn good manners, to acquire the necessary knowledge and to assert its domination. But nothing is natural, it is the consequence of a privileged situation and not the fruit of a purely personal merit.

On the other hand, what seems natural is that some humans seek dominance and power, and are willing to go to great lengths to achieve it, and then to legitimize their position and preserve it. Wealth is an essential component of power, because it allows one to coerce and subdue a large part of those who are not rich. The wealthy bourgeoisie of the 18th century thus succeeded in overthrowing the impoverished nobility, in order to take over the reins of the country, thus adding to its economic power the political power it lacked. In return, and after fierce struggles, it conceded greater equality of rights, but failed to guarantee it with adequate means. Now, without means, the equality of rights is limited to a right of principle, without effectiveness.

While undeniable progress has been made over the past two centuries, particularly in education and health care, thanks to more democratic institutions and the generalization of free or accessible public services, the same cannot be said for the business world. The right to equality remains a principle. As the saying goes, you only lend to the rich. Moreover, while the bourgeoisie advocates democracy for the people, it has no place in the economic world. In companies, the dictatorship of ownership is rampant. The shareholder decides, the employee obeys.

While inequalities have been decreasing for a century in our Western countries, they have been increasing for three decades. There is nothing natural about this. Economic inequalities have been increasing since the 1990s, since the fall of the Soviet bloc and the end of the employers' fear of communism, since the arrival of

3. THE RICH HAVE ALWAYS EXISTED BECAUSE INEQUALITY IS NATURAL

the third industrial revolution (the communications revolution) and its globalized and deregulated economic model, which is very profitable for the richest. Inequalities are the consequence of the omnipotence of "proprietarism", accentuated by a capitalism that has become globalized and financialized. The mobility of people and capital allows the richest to optimize their investments by reducing their constraints and obligations. And they benefit from it. Many economists and major international organizations agree. But nothing changes because the richest are the masters of the capitalist system. They take full advantage of it and are less and less forced to make concessions. Only the fear of a popular revolution would make them back down.

4. With hard work, anyone can become rich

The liberal doxa likes to put forward personal qualities in order to legitimize wealth: work, perseverance, talent, involvement. This statement is heavy with meaning. It makes the less wealthy feel guilty and justifies the wealth of the economic elite, who are supposed to have succeeded thanks to hard work and dedication. But is it true?

No, simply because work, alone, never brings wealth. The income from one's own work will never be enough to become rich, because it is subject to strong constraints. It is calculated by multiplying the working time by an hourly rate. But time is limited by nature (24-hour day, 365-day year, 50 years of working life at most), and competition from the vast labor market is fierce, putting pressure on hourly rates. This is why the differences in labor income are limited. They range from 1 to 9 times the minimum wage in France, far from the wealth gaps observed. The gaps are even smaller for a very large majority of the working population, since 70% of full-time workers earn between 1 and 2 times the Smic, 23% between 2 and 4 times the Smic; only 6% of workers earn between 4 and 9 times the Smic[6]. One percent

---

6. Insee/Dares, "Employment, unemployment, labor income", July 2020, and its detailed databases.

of the population earns more than 9 times the minimum wage, and most of this income is no longer earned from work, but from capital. This is mainly the case for large shareholders and owners who receive a much higher income from their capital than from their own work. While 20% of French households declare receiving dividends, 1.7% of tax households account for 97% of this financial income, and 0.1% for two-thirds[7]. The same is true for the private rental housing stock: 3.5% of households own 50% of privately owned rental housing[8].

There are also atypical personalities who benefit from notoriety. This is the case of celebrities, certain artists and sportsmen, and co-opted company directors who are entirely devoted to their shareholders. The "success" of these personalities is often put forward by the liberal doxa in order to demonstrate that any citizen can "succeed". However, these successes should be taken with caution. On the one hand, because notoriety is rare by definition. Only an extreme minority of the population can acquire substantial notoriety, sufficient to make the difference with the majority. It cannot therefore serve as a legitimate justification on a more "macro" scale, such as that of a country. The few poor people who have become famous and rich should not serve as role models for an entire country, since, structurally, their number will always be extremely limited. On the other hand, talent and fame alone do not guarantee wealth, because they also imply becoming "monetizable. How do you do this? Nothing happens by chance. This becomes possible when a talented celebrity becomes part of a "business", i.e. in a sector where capital has been invested in a significant way, generating high rents, part of which can be redistributed. But, make no mistake, in the end, it is the owners of this capital who will reap the largest share. In fact,

---

7. France Stratégie, "Comité d'évaluation des réformes de la fiscalité du capital", October 2021.
8. Insee, "France, social portrait", October 2021.

the rich use, or even exploit, talent as a marketing investment, in order to get richer. Famous singers keep the record and music business alive. Footballers, tennis players and golfers enjoy exorbitant incomes because these sports generate huge revenues for all investors (sponsors, media, merchandising…). Famous writers work for a few large publishing houses that now belong to a few billionaires. As for corporate executives, they are paid handsomely because they are the guarantors of the interests of the shareholders, whom they represent and protect, and not, per se, because they are talented. Conversely, a renowned biologist or sociologist, a talented chess player or javelin thrower, or an excellent leader of a major charity will never make a fortune.

The rich know how to be (somewhat) generous when they win. But this relative generosity always hides an exploitation of the work of others. Talents work hard to get a few crumbs (sometimes big ones in their own right), while investors share the biggest slice of the pie. Thus, the wealthy are quite willing to bring new "talent" to the forefront, as long as they make money for them, by selling music or books, by increasing the ratings of their media, by filling a stadium or a hall they sponsor. In fact, the goal of investors is not the success of the "talent" per se, but the additional profits it will generate. Even social media video influencers, who initially wanted to be independent, are caught up in the monetization of their fame. They manage to earn a lot of money when they turn into advertisers for big brands, participating in enriching especially the most fortunate.

And if some people manage to live well from their notoriety with the general public, in all independence, generally thanks to a real talent, they remain extremely marginal. Exceptions, in short, that confirm the rule.

5. Anyone can build a large estate

The defenders of our model like to tell (themselves) nice stories. With a little effort, everyone could build up a large fortune. All you have to do is work hard, save and be a little bit clever to make the most of your capital. This is easy to say when you are "well born", with an inherited fortune, relatives full of money... What about the others? According to the work of the economist Thomas Piketty[9], inheritance currently accounts for 75% of the wealth held, a weight that has been rising steadily since the 1970s (44% at that time). This level has become enormous! It means that only one quarter of the wealth is built by savings made during one's life. Moreover, according to the 2021 Forbes wealth ranking, 80% of French billionaires are heirs, an overwhelming share, as is generally the case in Western European countries. Meritocracy on the move or at half mast?

When you think about it, this is not surprising. Indeed, French households save 15% of their disposable income, or €3,500 per year per adult on average, of which one third is invested in financial assets and two thirds in real estate. Wealth seems far away with such small amounts. Of course, this average savings rate of 15 percent

---

9. Thomas Piketty, Le Capital au XXIe siècle, Seuil, 2013.

hides large differences within the French population[10]. The savings rate depends much less on consumption behavior (cicada or ant) than on income level. The poorest half of households generally do not manage to save, or save very little, because they do not have sufficient income to reconcile basic consumption and savings. Only the wealthiest 20 percent of the population save significantly: 30 percent of their disposable income, or an average of €13,000 per adult per year. However, even for the vast majority of them, these amounts are still insufficient to one day enter the rich class.

It is indeed the ownership of capital that makes wealth possible. Wealth feeds on itself. Inheritances and gifts currently account for 20 per cent of net disposable household income, up from 8 per cent in 1980; this share is expected to rise further in the future, to 25 to 30 per cent within 30 years[11]. This increase is explained by the fact that wealth is growing much faster than income. Indeed, since 1980, the disposable income of French households has increased by 86%, while wealth has increased fourfold! The problem inherent in this reality is that the distribution of wealth is extremely unequal, as is that of inheritances, much more so than that of income. Thus, one third of the French population inherits nothing, another third very little; on the other hand, 10% of heirs receive more than half of the national inheritance, with the first percentile receiving almost a quarter of the total. And since economic growth in Western countries is low and, conversely, the stock of pre-existing capital is enormous, it becomes very difficult to make a place for oneself in today's economic world, in contrast to the periods following the two world wars, when economic growth was high and the stock of pre-existing

---

10. Insee, "More savings among the wealthiest, more forced spending among the most modest," September 2020.
11. France Stratégie, "Can we avoid a society of heirs?", January 2017.

capital low. Is marriage the only opportunity left to become rich, as it was in the nineteenth century?

Wealthy families benefit from both inheritances and the annuities of their capital. Even more, they benefit from the continuous revaluation of their capital in a world where liquidity has become enormous. Contrary to the rhetoric of employers who value the talent of managers, this revaluation is in reality most often due to market conditions alone. We can cite the example of real estate owners who have benefited from an increase in the value of their property, without any particular intervention on their part. If this increase benefits all property owners, it is the owners of commercial and rental properties who benefit the most, to the detriment of the tenants, both individuals and businesses, whose rents are exploding. Another phenomenon, during the Covid-19 health crisis, the luxury, online commerce, Internet applications and health markets are doing wonderfully, making billions of dollars for their happy owners; supported by generous public aid and floods of liquidity from central banks during difficult times. This is how the fortune of the world's billionaires has increased by 45% over the two years 2020-2021 alone according to Forbes data, without any specific action on their part. French billionaires are not to be outdone, with a fivefold increase in their wealth in ten years, surpassing the Germans and the British. Meanwhile, in the midst of the pandemic, the "first in line" are on deck, with no increase in salary, while millions of people on our planet sink into poverty. Is everything okay?

Thus, when the economy is doing well, profits increase, driving up the value of companies. When there is an economic crisis, governments support companies and central banks pour billions of liquidity into them, mechanically increasing the value of assets. Thus, the owners always benefit. We are far from rewarding work and small savings.

6. The rich consume and invest

The rich consume, of course. Compared to a minimum wage earner, they consume much more. However, in proportion to their income, the rich consume little in reality, since the propensity to save increases with the level of income. Thus, while the poorest half of French people consume almost all of their income, the rich consume barely a third of it. If their spending can sometimes seem extravagant because of their luxury, and generous because they do not count, think again. On average, they spend little compared to their means. Of course, the rich remain courted clients, since they have substantial means, sometimes even astronomical. They can therefore afford to spend lavishly: villa, yacht, jet, dream vacation, domestic servants at home, personalized services, and even space tourism. A luxury that is frightening in terms of ecology, but surely "worth it"! On a micro level, the rich are still the customers of choice, since nothing is ever too expensive for them. However, the macroeconomic reality is less bright, with a reduced share of their income devoted to consumption. In order to revive the economy, it is therefore better to increase the income of modest households who will spend almost all of it, creating additional demand, and thus economic growth and jobs, rather than enriching the wealthy who will spend very little of this surplus income.

So, you might say, if they don't consume, the rich invest! This is indeed what we observed in the industrial capitalist model that developed from 1750 to 1975. In a relatively closed economy, the richest lent and invested in their country of origin, and companies hired locally. The share of wealth thus captured by the owners of capital fed the "real" economy through their investments. A trickle-down effect took place, even if this did not prevent extreme social inequalities, since the bourgeoisie has always been very reluctant to share. Their profits were reinvested but not much was redistributed in wages. It was social struggles that led to more redistribution. They were effective in a localized economy, with bosses who lived close to their companies and their employees.

But our national industrial capitalism has since evolved into a globalized and financialized capitalism. Investments have been relocated to low-cost countries in Eastern Europe and Asia. 600 billion euros have thus left France for investments abroad in recent decades[12]. This sum is not negligible, since it represents 20% of the net asset value of all French companies. The trend is identical in all Western countries: a total of 3.5 trillion in net investments have been relocated to emerging countries. So much money not used to create jobs in our countries. And this is only the tip of the iceberg. Much more colossal sums have left the "real" economy to join the financial sphere, which has become insatiable. In twenty years, 90,000 billion dollars have been placed on the world's derivative markets, 98% of which is speculation, as much as the total invested in the world's stock exchanges since their creation, totalling 20% of

---

12. Net outward and inward FDI (foreign direct investment) balance, based on data from the United Nations Conference on Trade and Development (UNCTAD), World Investment Report, 1990 to 2020.

the world's economic wealth net of debt. Shadow banks, those that are not regulated, benefit from this financialization of the economy, whose funds, created in the 1980s, have grown from $25,000 billion in 2002 to $141,800 billion in 2020[13]. The money is flowing, but, alas, no longer here.

Thus, the rents now captured by the owners of capital are no longer reinvested in Western countries. A small part of it goes abroad and a large part into the financial sphere... never to return. The richest people are progressively moving their wealth towards horizons that are more profitable for them, the emerging countries and finance. Their interests are opposed to those of our Western countries. They flout all their duties, with impunity! This explains why many coffers are empty, those of the working and middle class populations of Western countries and those of the States, while those of finance and the rich fill up, again and again. The world is overflowing with money and the majority no longer benefits from it. We are not in an economic crisis, it is our model that is in crisis.

---

13. Based on OFIs (other financial intermediaries) data from the Financial Stability Board, Global Monitoring Report on Non-Bank Financial Intermediation, December 2021.

7. Bosses create jobs

Employers often legitimize their dominant position by the role they play as job creators. We are somehow indebted to them because they create jobs. This is interesting, but is it true? Let's take a closer look at what has happened over the past 70 years. According to INSEE[14], there were 19.5 million jobs in France in 1949, totaling 43.25 billion hours of work. What is the situation today? France has 27 million jobs. So we have a net creation of 7.5 million jobs. We could therefore congratulate ourselves on this; except that these job creations have not been translated into the creation of working hours. In fact, our 27 million jobs total only 42.80 billion hours of work, or 450 million hours less than in 1949. The employers have not created a single hour of work in 70 years, despite all the state aid obtained to reduce the cost of labor.

Is this due to a lack of growth, as we sometimes hear? Well, no. In fact, economic growth has been prodigious over the period: an 8.5-fold increase in constant euros! Our annual gross domestic production (GDP) has increased by 750% in seventy years... for not one hour of work created.

---

14. According to INSEE's long time series covering 1949-2020: GDP, hours worked, employment and labor force.

Job creation comes solely from the reduction in working hours. We have gone from 45 hours of effective work per week in 1949 for full-time employees, with 2 weeks of paid vacation per year, to 36 hours of effective work per week (41 hours for fixed-term contracts) and 5 weeks of paid vacation currently[15]. Without a reduction in working hours, so decried by employers, France would have lost 300,000 jobs during this period, instead of creating 7.5 million. We would then be faced with a major problem, since the French working population has grown by 10 million people in the same period. The country would then have 11 million unemployed in category A (without a job), i.e. an unemployment rate of 37%, a totally unsustainable level!

How have we been able to generate so much wealth over this period without creating a single hour of work? Simply because of productivity gains. While national production has multiplied by 8.5, hourly productivity has multiplied by 8.6. In constant euros, it has gone from €6.25 in 1949 to €53.40 today, a level that is among the highest in the world. Thus, the economic growth, although spectacular over the period, has been achieved only by productivity gains, and not by an additional volume of work. This is not surprising when you know the business world. The objective of managers has never been to create jobs, but to maximize their profits. Sometimes, indeed, they hire in the short term to cope with an increase in orders. But in the longer term, management optimizes, rationalizes, mechanizes, automates... in order to reduce costs, especially personnel costs. When employers announce new jobs, they are usually the result of departures (retirements, resignations, layoffs). Hiring is always a default

---

15. At the same time, the number of part-time workers has risen sharply, but this decline in working hours has been offset by a decline in the number of self-employed workers without pay, even though they were working more. The recent rise of self-employment slightly alters this balance: the number of self-employed is rising again, but with a lower working time.

choice for employers. They agree to it when they cannot respond otherwise. And let's make no mistake, any reduction in the cost of labor will not change this logic of cost optimization, including that of labor. When employers talk about the need for competitiveness, we can say that they succeed, without creating jobs!

This reality is far from the whining speeches of the employers about our problems of competitiveness and their self-satisfaction about their role as job creators. Its incessant criticism of the cost of labor therefore seems fallacious when one observes the extent of productivity gains over the last seven decades. Could this be to avoid the real question of the distribution of productivity gains, between employees and shareholders? This is a subject that should probably be avoided, since the weight of wages is decreasing in favor of dividends. According to INSEE, wages represent 64% of value added in France, compared with 70% in the 1950s and 1960s, while the weight of dividends has doubled in the same period, from 6% of value added in the 1950s and 1960s to 12% today[16]. This evolution is not insignificant. It represents a transfer of wealth of €115 billion each year, an amount that corresponds to a salary increase of €400 per month for all employees, including all charges, or to the creation of 3.5 million full-time jobs at €1,500 net per month.

Our so-called problems of competitiveness and labor costs are nothing but subterfuges to increase profits and shareholder dividends. This strategy leads to wage moderation and low hiring. The crisis so often evoked is in reality a well-managed shareholder strategy, which benefits shareholders at the expense of employees and pensioners.

---

16. According to INSEE value added sharing data, excluding mixed income of sole proprietorships; and the INSEE analysis, "Le partage de la valeur ajoutée en France, 1949-2007," 2009. Note that the share devoted to investments and financial reserves has remained broadly stable over the period, at around 24%.

8. The rich are talented and deserving entrepreneurs

The entrepreneur represents the reference par excellence of the liberal doxa, with the symbol of the little guy in his garage who transforms the world and makes a fortune. Is this a reality or a myth?

Let's take the example of auto-entrepreneurship in France. This status was created in 2008 with the aim of encouraging the emergence of talent and "freeing up work". By the end of 2020, twelve years later, France had 1.9 million micro-entrepreneurs[17], representing 6% of the active population and half of the country's non-salaried jobs. The result thus seems honorable, but in reality hides the rise of a market of poor workers, with difficulties in integrating into conventional employment. 40% of them do not manage to generate any turnover from their activity, and for the 60% who do, their net income does not exceed 470 € per month on average. Half of them even earn less than 290 € per month. Only 10% manage to exceed the minimum wage[18]. We are far from the world of the rich, too often called "entrepreneurs". It is rather a quest for survival. The few

---

17. According to Urssaf, "Stat'ur conjoncture : les auto-entrepreneurs fin 2020", July 2021.

18. Insee, "Les revenus d'activité des non-salariés en 2015," February 2018.

success stories, so often put forward by the liberal doxa, hide a less glowing reality. The vast majority of entrepreneurs are not rich.

Let's take Bill Gates, the founder of Microsoft, and Mark Zuckerberg, the creator of Facebook, who are often cited as a reference for the successful young person. Are they just average students? When they made their name, they were both at Harvard, the most expensive university in the world, the most prestigious too, where the children of the rich are legion and business networks are omnipresent. These two students did not in fact succeed alone, in their garage. They benefited from an extremely favorable environment, with financial and commercial support that was beyond the norm. What would have happened if these students had come from a less fortunate university? Certainly nothing or almost nothing. To dare to evoke the image of a garage for Harvard students is distressing.

In fact, much more than individual talent, networks are the great determinants of success. The richest people are always very well off in this regard, because money attracts money and those who have it. As soon as opportunities to get rich present themselves, networks are activated to make their business grow. The rich know how to open the door to newcomers when it benefits them. But let's not be fooled. Doors often remain closed, or barely ajar. Family dynasties usually rule. The children of the richest enter one by one as leaders of the industrial and financial empire of their father and grandfather. We have seen this with the Bettencourt, Dumas, Wertheimer, Dassault, Bouygues, Louis-Dreyfus or Lacoste families. The movement continues, with more recently the Arnault, Mulliez, Pinault, Bolloré, Decaux, Michelin, Lagardère, or Ricard families. Is this a sign that talent is passed on from generation to generation, or rather that the rich have free rein to favor their offspring? What room is left for the children of the working and middle classes, apart from the fine speeches about equal opportunities and meritocracy?

If the working and middle classes can legitimately aspire to join the wealthy class, the wealthy class is not very accessible because the places are taken for the most part, with enormous means already committed. How to succeed today with little or no money? We are no longer in the post-war era of the 1920s or 1950s, when opportunities were plentiful in a context of strong economic growth and low capital investment. The stock of committed capital has grown from 3 times the country's income in those days to 7 times today. It is not easy to make a place for yourself when the heirs already occupy all the space. For the most motivated, the only option left is expatriation to emerging countries, where growth is stronger and capital investment lower.

In Western countries, the economic elite is omnipresent. This reproduction worthy of monarchies can even be observed among artists, where the need for capital is less, but where networks are essential. The children of actors, singers, producers, etc., take over the few available places that allow them to live honourably. The only thing left to give disadvantaged young people a chance is sport, because in this field, no network can substitute for real personal talent.

The success story of the talented small businessman is a myth that seeks to legitimize the wealth of the wealthy, which is based primarily on inheritance and a lucrative inner circle. The reality is that the vast majority of the rich are not entrepreneurs, but heirs and rentiers; that 99% of heirs will remain rich no matter how talented they are; that 99.99% of the poor will never be rich, no matter how talented they are.

9. The rich take risks and innovate

The market economy has the advantage of promoting entrepreneurial freedom and encourages motivation and personal initiative, which are sources of innovation and economic growth. Everyone can benefit from this if markets remain sufficiently open to newcomers. Yet, and this is the contradiction of liberals, we are told that deregulation is the way to free markets. However, these deregulations generally only lead to favouring oligopolies, i.e. a few large companies that are already present and have conquered a dominant place in their market. Today, 300 multinationals account for 30% of private-sector employment in France, and as many jobs with their suppliers[19]. Sixty percent of salaried jobs in the private sector are therefore directly linked to their activities and decisions. This shows that these 300 large companies dominate the national economy and influence the whole of society, especially since many small companies live off the consumption of these 60% of employees. However, these large companies are significantly owned by the wealthiest people. Their power is immense.

Certainly, some fortunes emerge when new markets emerge, as recently with the Internet or biotechnology. A few people manage

---

19. According to data from the Observatory of Multinationals.

to develop their business and get rich. But these are generally exceptions. France has 2.5 million very small businesses, 1.9 million self-employed entrepreneurs, 150,000 small and medium-sized enterprises (SMEs), 5,700 intermediate-sized enterprises (ETIs), 300 large companies in its private sector, and 1,750 public companies[20]. How many people will become rich by creating their own company in this magma of companies? In fact, success stories are very rare because they require a decisive competitive advantage, either a key patent or an outstanding specificity, which is very difficult to obtain and to develop. The examples often cited are the GAFAM (Google, Apple, Facebook, Amazon, Microsoft). However, these companies are atypical because they occupy a very dominant position in their market. In the IT and Internet sectors, network effects are at play, which has made it possible to make customers captive, with a concentration of supply... which poses the problem of free competition.

The current system does not encourage the emergence of new companies, except in emerging sectors. In fact, the dominant companies in place have no interest in taking risks through so-called "disruptive" innovations. However, it is these disruptive innovations that give rise to new products and markets, and that are reflected in the famous notion of "creative destruction" by the economist Joseph Schumpeter. Large companies are content with "continuity" innovations in order to improve their products, without destabilizing their market. This reality is found everywhere. The Internet was not created by the computer giants. Digital photography did not come from the big film companies. Snowboarding didn't come from ski manufacturers. The smartphone was born at Apple because the company was experiencing great difficulties in its compu-

---

20. Insee, "Les entreprises en France", December 2020.

ter market at that time. In fact, disruptive innovation almost always comes from young creators of startups or spin-offs, who are trying to enter a market and make a place for themselves, or sometimes from companies in difficulty that are trying to survive. The large dominant companies, on the other hand, adopt a rentier attitude. Their main objective is to preserve their assets by protecting their own interests. On the other hand, they will closely follow the technological advances of startups in order to buy them if necessary, or, failing that, to become associated with them. As for investment funds, their role remains marginal during startup launches. Funds dedicated to innovation or venture capital remain marginal. Startups find it very difficult to find financing at the beginning. They have to prove themselves first. Only once the innovation work is advanced, and if it proves promising, investors come in force.

Thus, the rich (investors and large companies) let the "small" ones innovate. Many of them will fail, often losing everything, their time, their money and their investments. And for the minority that will succeed in innovating, they will have to accept outside investors to grow or be bought out. This is the case for all health biotechs and Internet startups. Of course, the lucky founders and owners of these small companies will become very rich, but the innovations will then be taken over by multinationals and investment funds, and not always for the greatest benefit of the consumer, because if their impact on their business proves to be harmful, the innovation will be hijacked, bypassed or even silenced. In any case, only an extreme minority will be enriched, that of the owners of capital. The many researchers and inventors who will have participated in the adventure will only benefit from crumbs. Consumers will not always benefit from the best innovations, and in the best of cases, they will pay a high price for these innovations bought at a high price.

This is the sad world of financial capitalism, which is neither optimal nor fair in its rewards, privileging only the owners by providing them with an astronomical rent. People like Bill Gates are made heroes, ignoring all the favorable conditions from which they benefited, all those who participated without getting a reward to match, and the luck factor that often plays a determining role. This process of capture is unfair and yet generally accepted, or at least wrongly accepted.

10. The more rich people there are, the fewer poor people there are

By promoting the rise of a wealthy class, we are often led to believe that there are fewer poor people. However, the link between the two seems irrelevant. In twenty years, the purchasing power of the French has increased by 20% on average, while the value of their wealth has tripled over the period[21]. Yet, at the same time, France has more poor people (less than 50% of the median income): 5.6 million in 2019, compared to 4 million in the early 2000s. The fear of falling into poverty is growing: 11% of French people consider themselves poor and 25% fear becoming poor in the next few years[22]. The wealth of the poorest 20% of French people has decreased in 20 years, while the wealth of the 500 richest French people has increased tenfold, from 100 billion euros to nearly 1,000 billion euros. As for the United States, which has 40% of the world's millionaires and billionaires, it has a very high rate of poor people (18%), twice as high as in Europe. According to the United Nations Human De-

---

21. According to INSEE's long time series of disposable income and household wealth.
22. Center de recherche pour l'étude et l'observation des conditions de vie (Crédoc), "Améliorer la connaissance et le suivi de la pauvreté et de l'exclusion sociale," November 2021.

velopment Reports, inequality has been growing since the 1980s. 27% of the world's income growth over the last 35 years has benefited only the richest 1%, compared to only 12% for the poorest 50%. In all countries, the income share of the poorest half of the population has been declining since the 1980s, while the income share of the richest 10%, especially the richest 1%, has been rising steadily. Half of the increase in global wealth over the last 20 years has been accounted for by the richest one percent, while the poorest half of the population has not seen its wealth increase.

How can this dichotomy be explained? First, one more rich person does not usually lead to one less poor person. The correlation between rich and poor is rarely direct, as there are intermediate levels between the two. A poor person who becomes richer first joins the middle class, then eventually the affluent class before perhaps, in fact very rarely, entering the rich class. Enrichment is a stepwise process. A new rich person does not reduce the number of poor people. The founders of startups and spin-offs are usually senior executives or young graduates (5 or 8 years of higher education) and children of wealthy or even privileged families, rarely self-employed entrepreneurs from poor families or non-graduates.

Beyond this "micro" vision, there remains a major question on a more "macro" scale. Does the wealth of the dominant class make the wealth of a nation? Does it trickle down to the poor? The answer varies according to the situation. If the richest reinvest their rents (rents, interest, dividends) within the nation, by investing, hiring, increasing wages and paying taxes, then they participate in the collective enrichment. A trickle-down effect takes place. This phenomenon mechanically reduces poverty. On the other hand, when the captured rents go into the speculative financial sphere, into tax havens or abroad, the country as a whole becomes poorer because the "real" economy of the nation is drained of rents without being replenished by these same rents. Capital rents without reinvestment then accentuate poverty and inequality, as has been the case for the last thirty years in Western countries, explaining a feeling of impoverishment of the working and middle classes.

Conversely, the wealth of a nation always benefits the ruling class, through the additional rents it derives from its capital accumulated over decades at all levels of society (real estate, investments, corporations). The rich benefit from the economic growth of the country through the mechanical increase of rents, interests and dividends. During economic crises, if public interventionism helps the poorest, it also favours the richest, notably thanks to the liquidity of central banks, which leads to a surge in the value of existing assets, as in 2009 (subprime crisis) or in 2020 (health crisis).

Thus, not only does the increase in the number of multi-millionaires and billionaires that we are currently observing in no way mean a decrease in the number of poor people, but it even leads to an increase in poverty, since the rents are no longer reinvested in the economy. The process is accentuated by the increase in the value of assets, which is much higher than income, preventing all those who do not have capital from building it up. Real estate prices, both for houses and for commercial premises, are exploding, reducing a little more the access of the working and middle classes to property, or even simply to the financing of a rent for housing or the launching of a small business.

In order to reduce the number of poor people, only the growth and prosperity of the middle and wealthy classes are relevant. The challenge of a country's economic development lies not in the size and wealth of its rich class, but in that of its middle class and its wealthy class, because it is these classes that enable the economic

10. THE MORE RICH PEOPLE THERE ARE, THE FEWER POOR PEOPLE THERE ARE

take-off, thanks to the social (education, health) and economic (domestic demand) inclusion of the population. This is what happened in our developed countries in the 19th and 20th centuries and what can be observed in emerging countries that are experiencing an economic boom, such as China.

It is therefore not surprising that the wealth of the rich is exploding, while poverty is increasing in Western countries. This is not an inevitability. It is the result of a devastating mechanism, when rents are no longer reinvested in the "real" economy and liquidity abounds.

11. The rich pay a lot of taxes

The rich obviously pay more taxes than the middle class. However, what is the proportion of their income? Do they contribute to public finances to the extent of their means, through their taxes and social contributions? By earning 10 times more than the "average" French person, do the rich pay, at least, 10 times more than the average? The answer is no, for several reasons.

First, so-called progressive taxes, those whose tax rate increases with income or wealth, remain minor in France. Income tax, for example, represents only 7.5% of the country's public levies. And the progressivity of this tax has been gradually reduced. When the income tax was created in 1914, the richest 1% paid 99% of it, compared to 30% today. As for the solidarity tax on wealth (ISF), it represented only 0.5% of national levies in 2017, a level reduced to 0.2% since Emmanuel Macron's reform transforming the ISF into the tax on real estate wealth (IFI). Then there remains the progressive inheritance tax, which totals only 1.3% of public levies. Overall, 91 per cent of public levies are in fact proportional, either to income, such as social security contributions and CSG-CRDS (50 per cent of levies) and corporate taxes (11 per cent), or to expenditure, such as VAT (16 per cent), taxes on petroleum products, insurance, electricity, cigarettes and alcohol (7 per cent)[23].

Secondly, there are many tax niches that allow for significant tax reductions, especially when one has significant means. The 471 existing tax niches in France total 91 billion euros[24]. This is as many tax reductions from which the richest people largely benefit. Moreover, taxes on capital income are lower than those on labor income. The argument often put forward is to avoid double taxation, first on labour and then on the products of savings from labour. If this principle applies to small savers who work, it should not logically apply to annuitants who live from their capital and not from their work (or only marginally). Indeed, capital income is not subject to social security contributions, except for CSG-CRDS. It is true that capital income does not provide social rights to its owners, but in fact, their capital provides a right to an annuity ad vitam æternam. Moreover, the tax rate on capital income is now capped at 30% of income since the introduction of the flat tax in 2017 by Emmanuel Macron. Finally, financial arrangements to "optimize" one's taxes are multiplying for the wealthiest and large companies. Globalization and tax havens are opening up numerous opportunities for individuals and companies with money, some of which are simply playing with the law.

Finally, our tax model is not very progressive. Income tax represents on average only 18% of the taxable income (net income) of the richest, a level not much higher than that of an average executive. And this share is likely to be lower if undeclared income is included. Thus, the income tax burden has been reduced almost continuously over the last thirty years, according to the Conseil des prélèvements

---

23. Insee, "General government expenditure and revenue in 2018," March 2020.
24. According to the appendix to the 2022 budget bill, "Assessment of Ways and Means.

obligatoires[25]. So let's stop decrying the excessive volume of taxes in France, at least for the rich, by recalling that the marginal income tax rate reached 80% in the United States from 1934 onwards, during the Great Depression, and then 91% during the Second World War. According to the United Nations, France has become one of the least redistributive countries in Europe[26].

Thus, the French rich finance the public coffers relatively little through their taxes and social contributions. While the rate of public deductions on the middle and wealthy classes is around 50% of their total income (gross income), it falls below 40% for the richest. The rate of public deductions on the richest is even lower than that of the working class, which does not pay income tax. The latter contribute up to 40% of public financing via their social contributions and the many taxes they pay (VAT, fuel, energy, tobacco, alcohol, etc.). In proportion, the poor therefore contribute more to public and collective financing than the rich. How is this possible? Simply because globalization has made it possible for the rich and large companies to be mobile and thus to impose reductions on all progressive taxes, under penalty of expatriation, which they do not fail to do, at least in part, since many countries are very understanding towards this coveted population. Tax rates on income, inheritance, profits and capital gains have been falling all over the world for thirty years, gradually reducing the resources of public authorities. But where has our tax money gone, ask citizens? Some of it has disappeared, since the rich are paying less and less. The current tax frustration can be explained by the growing tax inequity.

---

25. "Compulsory taxes on households: progressivity and redistributive effects," May 2011.
26. United Nations Development Programme (UNDP), Human Development Report 2019 - item 7.3, Differences in the redistributive effect of taxes and direct transfers in Europe.

12. The rich are generous benefactors

Patronage is becoming increasingly popular with large companies and the wealthy. It allows to financially support many projects in the fields of health, education, culture and ecology. Patronage is based on an altruistic approach and its action has a positive impact on society as a whole, to fight against poverty, the difficulties of disability or integration, or environmental degradation.

However, on closer inspection, we quickly realize that the approach goes far beyond mere philanthropy. First of all, patronage benefits from particularly advantageous tax deductions: it is a way to give its contributors a very rewarding image at little cost. When you give 10 €, it costs you a maximum of 4 €. This is much more interesting than advertising. Moreover, sponsorship has the advantage of creating an identity around a theme and certain values, and of involving a group. The underlying goal is to improve the company's image, while encouraging the involvement and loyalty of its network (employees, customers, partners, etc.) through actions that stimulate support for its brand or name. Given the market value of the image of major brands, we can better understand the importance of this approach. The Kantar Brand study[27] estimates the value of the

---

27. 2021 edition of the Kantar BrandZ ranking that evaluates brands.

top 50 French brands at 325 billion dollars and the top 100 global brands at 7,100 billion dollars. The brand has become a key element in the value of a company. For any shareholder, valuing his brand is therefore valuing his assets. And since the State finances *at least* 60% of it, sponsorship is a godsend. Sponsorship is therefore a good complement to advertising, adding a societal and unifying notion, marked by virtue. Advertising has already evolved in this direction, focusing more on the image of the brand than on the intrinsic qualities of the products.

To go even further, there is nothing better than to create a foundation to better structure one's philanthropic actions. Foundations have experienced a meteoric rise, first in the United States, then in the rest of the world. They generally bear the name of their founder, a large company or a wealthy person, offering legitimacy and reputation. Who hasn't heard of Bill and Melinda Gates' or Warren Buffet's foundations and their billions? However, the sums paid out are very modest on a country scale. The funding of American foundations, even though they are the richest, represents less than 1% of American public spending. There is a lot of talk about them even though their funding remains extremely marginal. Generally, far from the millions or even billions raised by foundations, only the income from their investments is spent. A lot of communication for little funding is the art of the rich: communication to enhance the value of low funding and to hide the fact that they participate less and less in public services and benefits. The return on investment of foundations is very profitable. Foundations bring to their founder an aura and an extraordinary capacity of influence.

Moreover, the approach of foundations, at first sight altruistic, often hides private interests, like a modern lobbying. They allow the general public as well as elected politicians to give an institutional basis to an approach that is in fact individual. The voice of the rich is thus heard much more readily through their foundations. They also allow to reinforce the influence and business networks during sumptuous charity evenings, where the guests are handpicked and benefit from tax reductions. What more could you ask for? Private foundations are thus progressively immersing themselves in society, a sign of the power acquired by the wealthiest. They are even beginning to overshadow non-governmental organizations (NGOs). They hasten to intervene during humanitarian disasters in order to win new contracts for reconstruction. We find ourselves in a process of hidden privatization, to the detriment of public intervention and civil society - let's remember: at little cost. In fact, they are above all a way of influencing society and winning new contracts.

This is not surprising. Numerous studies show that people's empathy decreases as their wealth increases. Paul K. Piff, a professor at Berkeley, a university at the forefront of social psychology, shows that as "a person's level of wealth increases, their capacity for compassion and empathy decreases, even as their feelings of entitlement, reward, and self-interest ideology increase[28]. In fact, one only has to look at the lifestyle of the wealthiest and their impact on the environment to understand their interest in social and environmental causes. A rich person emits 70 times more CO_2 than a poor person. How many times more for the billionaires, with their private jet, their yacht, their luxury villa? It doesn't seem to matter.

Even if some actions were motivated by a real humanistic generosity, they would only be charity. But let us never forget that charity is no substitute for social justice.

---

28. Paul K. Piff, Higher social class predicts increased unethical behavior, Proceedings of the National Academy of Sciences (PNAS), February 2012.

13. We all want to be rich

To begin with, let's specify that the notion of "rich" is perceived differently by everyone. For many French people, it means an income of around 5,000 euros per month. For a minority, it can be much more. We can already see a confusion between affluence and wealth. In fact, many of us would like to have comfortable means to live properly. But do we really want to be "rich" in the sense of "very rich"? According to a survey by sociologist Rainer Zitelmann[29], 30% of French men and 24% of French women think that being rich is personally important. This result, which is in line with the European average, shows that we do not all aspire to become rich, and certainly very few want to become very rich.

Material wealth in fact responds to various objectives, which we must distinguish in order to avoid any confusion. Its first objective is to protect, by ensuring one's physiological needs (food, shelter, clothing, transportation...), without major constraints, without having to count on every moment. This objective is totally legitimate. The second objective of material wealth is to be able to please oneself and one's loved ones, by offering oneself goods and services for

---

29. Seven-country survey study, "Attitudes toward the Rich," Economic Affairs, May 2021.

comfort and leisure. This daily comfort is a source of satisfaction, such as a dinner in a restaurant, a weekend in a beautiful place, a vacation with a change of scenery, leisure activities, festive moments, a nice house, beautiful furniture, quality accessories for one's activities, etc. Human needs go beyond the scope of basic needs. Many of us therefore aspire to this financial ease, even if the ecological question now invites itself into the legitimacy of this approach by pertinently raising the question of the desired and desirable utility of certain expenses, and by privileging quality over quantity. Its third objective is the freedom that a certain financial ease confers to accomplish personal projects. It helps to realize them, thanks to both the material and human means that can be made available and the time that can be freed up to devote to them. This objective is also legitimate and healthy.

Material wealth then covers two other, more subjective objectives: a social objective, more or less conscious, and self-esteem. Beyond the personal satisfaction linked to the use of goods and services, wealth represents a strong sign of social success. These two objectives take a very different place depending on each person's personality, values and social environment. They can be healthy, as long as they remain measured. They can also lead to important deviations, some of which prove to be unhealthy.

We find them in the famous pyramid of needs of the psychologist Abraham Maslow, with, from the base to the top: physiological needs, security, belonging and love, esteem and, finally, self-fulfilment. Financial wealth seems to be enough to meet most of these goals. So why do some people want to become rich? We are probably entering into more subjective reasons. The problem would mainly come from a perversion of the objectives of social recognition and self-esteem. In our societies where success and power come through money, the need for social recognition and self-esteem often requires a lot of money; even more so when power becomes a goal. All people in search of power and narcissistic compensation will logically be incited to get rich in an inordinate way. The problem is not so much that there are deviant people (there always will be), but that our capitalist society encourages this perversion. Greed is stimulated, even exalted, instead of being fought and curbed. The most narcissistic and cynical individuals flourish in this competition exacerbated by the capitalist system, where the power of money shines and makes one shine, where all tricks are allowed to succeed.

It is essential to dissociate the means from the objective. If wealth can make people dream, it is not so much the money itself that is sought after, because it is only a means, but rather the freedom it can provide. Thus, if many would gladly accept a providential gain of money, in the lottery for example, few people seem ready to do anything to become rich. Only the most neurotic lead a frantic race towards more and more money, using all means to achieve it, abusing a hard-won power. The worst thing is that the whole society suffers from their neurotic race.

There are probably many more of us who aspire to just the opposite, to a fairer and healthier society, where personal fulfilment and financial ease would have their place alongside common projects; where economic dynamism would not be at odds with the notions of equity, solidarity and balanced development. According to a survey[30], 80% of French people would be in favor of devoting more resources to public services, 73% would be in favor of reducing income disparities and 69% would be in favor of greater redistribution.

---

30. Crédoc/Ademe report, "Focus sur les aspirations vis-à-vis notre modèle de société", October 2021.

The capitalist system incites us to lead a race to desire, in an alienating servitude, making us believe that our well-being lies in material wealth, because this enriches and legitimizes it. We do indeed need wealth, but certainly not to feed excessive egos. Above all, they should allow us to offer a decent life to the greatest number of people and give us the means to collectively take up challenges, by rediscovering the sense of living well together, with respect for each other, our environment and our planet.

14. Money makes you happy

Money, in our so-called modern societies, allows, at least partially, to be accomplished, because it opens the field of possibilities. Indeed, the lack of money hinders the realization of one's personal projects, and therefore one's happiness. But does money bring happiness?

Money allows us to get out of misery, and therefore out of a certain misfortune. The fight against poverty is essential. However, happiness is not limited to "unhappiness". It is based on a state of well-being, resulting from an alchemy between several ingredients leading to personal fulfillment within society: health, love, pleasant living conditions, fulfilling social and professional relationships, emancipating freedom. On this basis, money can certainly contribute to positively nourish the ingredients of happiness, by facilitating the conditions of their obtention. However, money does not guarantee it. Moreover, wealth does not necessarily offer more happiness than financial ease. It even generates additional risks and difficulties.

Indeed, all studies show that monetary satisfaction is real. The happiness of a population automatically increases with economic development. The Danes are globally happier than the Somalis.

However, marginal satisfaction decreases until it becomes zero, or even negative, beyond a certain threshold. Thus, an increase in monthly income from €1,000 to €2,000 will give a French person a great deal of satisfaction because it will help him or her to better meet basic needs. An additional income increase of €1,000 will bring less satisfaction, although still important, because it will allow to meet secondary needs, comfort and ease. The additional gains will then generate less and less additional well-being. Beyond a threshold of around 6,000 euros per month, "monetary satisfaction" could even become negative, according to the Nobel Prize in Economics, Angus Deaton[31]. Indeed, the difficulties of earning more would become greater than the satisfaction brought by the additional gain.

However, the quest for wealth does not always stop because, if we are not careful, expectations tend to evolve in the process of getting rich, demanding more and more luxuries and pleasures, ultimately generating more stress than satisfaction. It is an unhealthy and incessant hedonistic quest that we should be wary of. The apparent ease that money induces, too much money, is perverse because it grants a power that distorts relationships with others. It generates docility in those around us, even submission. Degrading behaviors then become the norm. And yet, they do not make anyone grow. Wealth infantilizes because it gives the unhealthy power to keep one's childishness with magnificence. An unenviable situation indeed. Moreover, wealth can quickly become a straitjacket and a source of worries and fears: of being robbed, robbed or swindled, of being surrounded by profiteers, of losing one's social position and, paradoxically, of being unloved in a world where the rich remain and will always remain a minority.

---

31. See in particular Angus Deaton's The Great Escape: Health, wealth and the origin of inequality, Princeton University Press, 2013.

Less than 3% of Europeans consider the rich to be honest. Finally, the quest for power and money has the unfortunate tendency to destructure human relations and social foundations, leading to all kinds of abuses: impoverishment and precariousness of a part of the population, delinquency, drugs, loss of confidence in institutions and the future. Society suffers serious collateral effects from these perverse behaviors, favoring abuse of power, predatory and domineering competition, rather than cooperation and trust, since the efforts required to become rich quickly prove insufficient to bear them alone. Additional work is no longer sufficient beyond a certain level of income. It is then necessary to resort to rent, the only way to generate a large income. And in the capitalist system, the owner is in a strong position to pass on the necessary efforts to others (employees, suppliers and customers). Our model is doubly perverse. Not only does it encourage the aberrant pursuit of wealth, but it also provides the means for wealthy owners to abuse their power by exploiting others to increase their wealth. All of this is done with the sole purpose of satisfying the base power instincts of a minority, which is absolutely not necessary for personal happiness, let alone collective happiness.

Thus, if financial ease contributes to happiness, wealth feeds our most vile natural inclinations, making the rich person a dopamine addict with easy pleasures, as opposed to real happiness which is based on serotonin. But too much dopamine naturally destroys serotonin. It's a vicious circle: when dopamine takes over, we always need more to compensate for the lack of serotonin. It is easy to understand why the rich never have enough and are ready to do anything to amass more and more money, beyond what is reasonable. If money contributes to happiness, wealth does not make happiness, it becomes a drug.

15. Wealth is the main driver of entrepreneurial drive

Money, i.e. income and income prospects, is without context a motivating factor in one's work. Everyone wants to be rewarded for their work in a way that is both decent and commensurate with their merit. Income from work is a legitimate reward for one's efforts, time, energy and involvement, and the skills one brings to the job. It plays an essential role, both in terms of meeting material needs and social recognition.

However, money is not the only factor in motivation and job satisfaction. According to a survey on the quality of life of employees at work[32], "recognition of the work done" is at the top of the podium, followed by "the nature of the responsibilities and missions entrusted" and "relational quality and pleasant work environment". Remuneration only comes in fourth place, tied with "opportunity to progress in skills and responsibilities". Few employees are willing to leave a good, well-paid job for a crappy one with better pay. However, the reverse is much more common.

---

32. Deloitte and Cadremploi.fr survey, "Quality of life at work: and happiness?", April 2015.

In fact, compensation is a major source of dissatisfaction when it is not considered commensurate with one's involvement. And many employees are dissatisfied with their pay. 7 out of 10 employees don't feel they are getting the recognition they deserve. The lower you are in the hierarchy, the less you feel recognized. This situation can be explained by the fact that capitalism privileges economic utility and not social utility, offering much higher remuneration to those who enrich the shareholders. Tax lawyers and restructuring or marketing specialists who zealously serve the interests of the owning minority earn much more than nurses, firefighters or personal assistants who, above all, serve the community. This paradox is more and more difficult to live with, and rightly so, since the vast majority of the population only wants to participate in the needs of the community through an identified and meaningful role, with quality working conditions and a decent salary. Nothing extraordinary then. We are far from the desire for fortune that the liberal doxa promotes.

What about entrepreneurs, business creators? Is their motivation to become rich? Without this desire for wealth, would there be no more entrepreneurs? However, studies[33] are, once again, unambiguous on the subject. They reveal that entrepreneurs have a thirst for independence and freedom through their activity, and that they are ready to take risks to become autonomous. The financial aspect is far from being the primary motivation for the entrepreneur, even if he obviously wants to be able to live decently from his project. Insee surveys[34] on the motivations of entrepreneurs reveal that the desire to be independent was a factor for 61%

---

33. "What are the motivations of entrepreneurs today?", Dynamique Mag, September 2020.

34. Insee, "Les créations et créateurs d'entreprises en 2010: situation initiale, situation en 2013 et en 2015," SINE survey, May 17, 2017.

of them, while the taste for entrepreneurship and the desire to face new challenges came in second place with 44% of responses. The prospect of increasing one's income only comes in third place, with 27%. The reality of motivations thus appears far removed from the wealth promotion distilled by our leaders, such as Emmanuel Macron in Las Vegas in January 2015, who proclaimed, "We need young French people who want to become billionaires." What young person goes into entrepreneurship really hoping to become a billionaire?

This encouragement to get rich actually serves to legitimize the fortunes of the ruling class, by making us believe that many of us dream of wealth. By titillating our baser instincts of greed, this caste seeks to make us adhere to the right to wealth. Surveys show, however, that this is not a shared objective. Fortune is not the main motivation for a successful life, and fortunately so, because the chosen ones are rare, as we know, at least for those who are not born with a silver spoon in their mouth. Professionally, the most important thing is to have a job that is both useful and interesting, with a certain degree of autonomy, that will allow you to achieve personal fulfillment and blossom, by actually earning a decent or even comfortable income, commensurate with your skills and involvement.

Conversely, we observe the growing importance for entrepreneurs to include values in their project: technical know-how, attachment to the territory, social ties, going beyond the sole notion of profits. The notions of meaning, of feeling like an actor, of equity and of service to others are becoming increasingly important in an economic system that is felt to be dehumanized. Far from the quest for fortune, the objective of a majority seems to be the search for meaning. It would therefore be salutary to rebalance the hierarchy of values in our society, to favor more the values of self-transcendence, such as benevolence (loyalty, helpfulness, honesty, forgiveness) and universalism (peace, wisdom, justice, harmony, nature), taking up those of the psychologist Shalom Schwartz[35], and a little less those of self-assertion, such as power (authority, wealth) and success (competence, ambition)

35. Shalom Schwartz, "Core Person Values: Theory, Measurement, and Applications," French Sociological Review, 2006/4, vol. 47, pp. 929-968.

16. The right to wealth is freedom

Freedom is considered a fundamental value, and rightly so. One only has to listen to those who lack it or have lacked it to realize this. Nevertheless, the extent of personal freedom must remain circumscribed to that which preserves the freedom of others. Our societies have placed many limits on our personal freedoms. The Covid-19 health crisis is a perfect example. For a long time now, limits have been placed on the use of private property. The use of a car or a boat, for example, requires compliance with very strict regulations. Owning land requires maintenance, occupying a home induces obligations, as does running a business. Being a property owner does not mean doing whatever you want within your property. There are rules to respect, which no one is supposed to ignore. They are governed by codes: highway code, navigation code, civil code, town planning code, commercial code, labor code, etc.

On the other hand, the right to own knows no limits in our society. A person can thus accumulate without end, whether it be land, real estate, investment funds, shares in companies. This is astonishing because we can and should ask whether this freedom to accumulate without limits, during our lifetime and by inheritance, does not impede the freedom of others.

Freedom of fortune is often justified by the freedom to undertake. Creating and developing a business, seizing an opportunity to offer a new product or service is a risk that must be motivated and rewarded. However, entrepreneurial freedom is very relative in reality, since it requires adequate means to achieve it. Thus, if the market economy has the advantage of being in constant evolution, creating new opportunities, certain conditions are essential to seize them, especially for large-scale projects likely to bring important gains. It is generally necessary to have technical, financial and commercial knowledge and skills, funds to invest, networks to make one's innovation known, to develop it, to market it, and a lot of time... Not everyone has this, at least in comparable proportions. Courage, audacity and effort, so extolled by liberals, are generally not enough.

This is all the more true since the market economy also has the disadvantage of generating adjustment costs during its continuous evolution. It is essential to adapt, but this comes at a cost, in terms of production capital and "human" capital, and this cost is all the heavier the less diversified the capital held. This is particularly true for employees, the self-employed and small businesses. The small entrepreneur takes significant risks, often investing all of his capital. In case of failure, the personal cost is very high. Employees also play a big role, as they usually only have their human capital to enter the world of work, i.e. their education and professional experience. Thus, when an employee loses his or her job, the stakes for him or her are threefold: to find a job quickly because it is his or her only source of income (apart from a right to unemployment benefit limited in time), but also a job in his or her field in order to preserve his or her human capital, and in geographical proximity, otherwise he or she will have to assume long trips or a costly move, financially and above all socially (his or her professional network is often local). We can better understand the distress of employees who are suddenly laid off and the fears linked to the risks of not finding a job of the same type and in the same place. On the other hand, the wealthiest will have the means to diversify their investments, allowing them to be proportionally less impacted by the costs of adjustment, and to have reserves if needed, in order to face the necessary adjustments, without risking losing everything.

So what kind of freedom are we talking about and for whom? Freedom in a complex system requires a great deal of autonomy, especially financial autonomy, even though the situation is currently totally unequal between people, rich or poor, and companies, large or small. The rich have much greater mobility of their financial and human capital, allowing them to take advantage of the opportunities offered by the market economy. The others, whose capital is much less mobile, are much more strongly affected by the negative aspects of the adjustments to be made, without being able to take advantage of the opportunities that arise. This model mechanically leads to virtuous circles for the better off and vicious circles for the others, the latter even becoming prey for the larger ones: precarious employees, butchered companies, pillaged territories. We find again the predatory behavior of capitalist competition, which is in no way akin to freedom, but rather to an exploitation that does not speak its name.

17. Too much government and taxes prevent you from getting rich

A liberal vision has progressively imposed itself with a well-trained discourse. The French state would squander our wealth, with 56% of national production (GDP) devoted to public spending, and would prevent citizens from getting as rich as they could and should.

This is a mistaken view. First of all, part of public spending is self-financed by own resources, leading to a real need for public financing of 48% of GDP, of which about 3% is the public deficit (excluding the crisis period), which means that taxes are actually 45% of GDP, not 56%.

Moreover, most of this 56 percent of GDP is in benefits, not expenditures. They are managed by public bodies but feed into the private market economy. For a total of 35 per cent of GDP at present, they are made up of retirement pensions (14 per cent of GDP, most of which is spent on consumption), the cost of health care, disability and sickness (9 per cent of GDP, financing hospitals, clinics, pharmacies, pharmaceutical companies, ambulance services and the health professions), interest charges on the public deficit (2 per cent of GDP), the cost of health care (2 per cent of GDP) and the cost of health care services (2 per cent of GDP).), interest charges on the public deficit (2% of GDP financing the financiers), and various aids for 10% of GDP[36]. It should be noted that less than half of these aids concern individuals (unemployment benefits, family aids, housing aids, activity bonuses and minimum social benefits), while more than half concern companies. The "crazy money" in aid, to use Emmanuel Macron's words, is in fact dedicated more to companies than to citizens. It is surprising that so little mention is made of this distribution of aid, which is very favorable to companies. The situation is different in Germany. While assistance to individuals is comparable to that of France (4.5 per cent of GDP), it is much lower for companies (2.9 per cent of GDP)[37].

In reality, public service expenditure itself only represents 21% of GDP, and has been decreasing slightly since 1980 (23% of GDP under Valéry Giscard d'Estaing). And a quarter of this expenditure feeds private companies, through public tenders: 170,000 private companies work for the State and local authorities (supplies, services, construction sites, public service delegations...). These contracts have often allowed large companies to consolidate their commercial and financial power, and to enrich their owners, such as the famous Bouygues and Dassault. Purely public spending therefore represents only 16% of GDP, a rather moderate level, far from the 56% generally mentioned! It finances internal public investments and the salaries of public employees (5.4 million people, of whom 70% are civil servants[38]) who work in services that are essential to the community: education (1.3 million people), hospitals

---

36. Insee, "General government expenditure, revenue and borrowing requirement," May 2020, and data from the statistical service of the Ministry of Social Affairs (Drees) and from Eurostat.
37. According to data from Ceo-Rexecode, "The public spending gap between France and Germany," Working Paper No. 69, June 2018.
38. Local Government Directorate, "Local Government in Numbers 2019," June 2019.

(1.2 million), territorial technical functions (0.9 million), security (0.7 million), administration, economics and finance (0.7 million), social and medico-social services (0.4 million), and entertainment, sport and culture (0.2 million).

It is true that public services have increased over the past 40 years in France, from 23% of GDP in 1980 to 35% today. However, this is in no way a question of waste, but rather the consequence of an aging population. Retirement and health care expenses are mechanically increasing, which is a major challenge for our society. However, if the temptation is strong to reduce our taxes and levies in order to "free up energy", as the liberals say, we must ask ourselves the right questions. Do we want to reduce the means dedicated to our pensions, to health, to education, to security or to our public infrastructures? And if we privatize these services, will we really pay less for comparable services? Let's be careful, because the opposite is often the case. Privatizations generate additional costs due to the multiplication of actors, because private companies have to create commercial services, resort to advertising, manage customer and employee turnover, while economies of scale are reduced and private shareholders demand dividends. The unavowed objective of the rich is to take over new sectors by privatizing them, even though the logic of the private market has serious limits in all sensitive sectors such as health, education, energy, security and infrastructure, in order to simply increase their wealth and power a little more.

No, public spending in no way prevents people from getting rich, at least collectively. They guarantee a minimum of free services accessible to all, of redistribution and protection. They are the foundation of our life together. Moreover, public authorities play an essential role in the elaboration of norms and rules in order to guarantee a minimum of equality between citizens and companies, through

17. Too much government and taxes prevent you from getting rich

the respect of common rules, without which our world would become a jungle, offering all power to the strongest. The State is the guarantor of the elaboration of the law and of its respect, in order to protect everyone, especially those in an unfavorable situation. Public interventionism is not opposed to the development of a country, nor to that of companies, quite the contrary. It offers many essential services and common rules that form a healthy basis for true development, favorable to the working, middle and wealthy classes, provided, at least, that it remains fully at the service of the general interest, and not of its dominant minority.

18. Capitalism has brought the world out of poverty

The question of the role of capitalism in the development of our societies is essential. Indeed, if this model has allowed and still allows to improve the situation of a large majority of the population on a long term, any questioning becomes inappropriate. So what about it?

Capitalism began to take off in mid-18th century England and gradually spread throughout the world. For its advocates, it is capitalism that has enabled the economic boom that the world has seen, leading to an increase in life expectancy and standard of living, increased access to education and health care, and a decrease in extreme poverty. This overall improvement, even if it has been uneven over time and is still geographically very heterogeneous, is real. However, two major elements significantly temper the benefits of capitalism.

First of all, the results obtained are disappointing compared to the increase in wealth observed. Extreme poverty has certainly been reduced, but not by much. On earth, 700 million people live on less than $1.90 a day, that is, nearly 10% of the world's population lives in total destitution[39]. And extreme poverty is much higher if we consider, as the United Nations promotes, a more relevant threshold of subsistence situated between $3.20 and $5.50 per person per day depending on the country. Thus, 2.4 billion people would still not be able to meet their basic needs, i.e. one third of the world's population! The UN also warns about the continuous increase in undernourishment, even though the world has never been so rich. In 2018, 822 million people were suffering from hunger and 1.3 billion people did not have regular access to nutritious and sufficient food[40]. And the situation is getting worse since the Covid-19 health crisis. In developed countries, inequalities are increasing, with the impoverishment of the working class and part of the middle class. A whole fringe of the global population is therefore not benefiting from global economic growth, even though it is vigorous (3% per year on average since the 1980s).

On the other hand, this economic growth is accompanied by social and environmental destructuring. According to the same United Nations Development Report, water supply is still a challenge for 4 billion people, while each year more than 200 million people are affected by natural disasters, 12 million hectares are affected by drought and desertification, 24 billion tons of fertile land are lost to erosion, 7 million net hectares of tropical forest disappear, 250 million tons of unrecycled plastics cause serious damage to the fauna and flora, both terrestrial and marine. And the list goes on: a sharp decrease in biodiversity (fauna and flora), impoverishment and contamination of land, rivers and seas, air pollution, global warming and climate change, etc. Moreover, progress in education seems more relative than it appears, because if the rate of schoo-

---

39. World Bank, Poverty and Shared Prosperity 2020.
40. United Nations Development Programme (UNDP), Human Development Report 2018, February 2019.

ling is progressing, the means granted to the school (teachers, students, infrastructures and governance) remain largely insufficient in many places to ensure a correct education. The results of capitalism are therefore mixed, accentuating tensions and violence, generating trafficking, banditry, guerrilla warfare, fundamentalism and uncontrolled mass migration.

Then an essential question arises: does the progress made really come from the capitalist model or is it linked to other factors? To understand this, let's look at some history. The market economy developed very gradually over many centuries. It then evolved into industrial capitalism during the 18th century. In France, as in all Western countries, the state became stronger and more interventionist, particularly in the 20th century, by introducing increasingly strict rules and standards, investing in essential sectors (transport, energy, education, health, etc.) and implementing redistribution policies. This state interventionism has clearly contributed to the economic development of Western countries. The other countries, which remained colonies or had no state structure, did not experience the same growth. The economic and social development of the West is therefore mainly due to the combination of a market economy and strong public regulation, generating efficiency and equity. The concomitance of these two factors has facilitated the emergence and the diffusion of productions and innovations, thanks to an efficient redistribution within the society, stimulating the demand for goods (material progress) and services (education, health, culture...). The role of capitalism in this development has remained, at best, marginal.

The recent rise of globalized financial capitalism, since the 1980s, has even contributed negatively to economic development, by reducing the impact of government regulatory policies. This largely explains our underperformance over the past thirty years. Conversely, China, which has succeeded in opening up its economy to the market economy while introducing numerous regulations (accompanied by some very worrying abuses of individual rights), has experienced real economic development by creating a real middle class.

19. Capitalism is the only viable economic model

Outside of capitalism, there is no salvation, we are often told. This point deserves to be explored in greater depth, without falling into the easy and simplistic shortcut of communism as the only alternative.

Let's look for a moment at what capitalism means. Capitalism is a very particular form of market economy, conferring an exclusive and full right of ownership on the owner of a good or a company. This right of ownership encompasses three dimensions: usus, the right to use it; abusus, the right to dispose of it, i.e., to transform it, to destroy it in whole or in part, or to transfer it to a third party; and fructus, the right to reap the fruits of the property. Rules exist to regulate the exercise of these rights. However, they remain sufficiently moderate not to call into question the rights themselves. The capitalist system thus grants decision-making power to the owners, in particular to the shareholders of companies who decide on management choices (usus) and strategy (abusus), and freely dispose of the profits generated (fructus).

In the face of the hegemonic power of the owners of capital, successive regulations made it possible to (partially) rebalance the forces at work during the phase of industrial capitalism. The trade unions contributed to favourably reinforcing the balance of power between the owners of capital and the employees. The public authorities also corrected the balance of power between private actors, by proposing laws and regulations that protected actors in an unfavourable position: tenants, borrowers, employees, minority shareholders, subcontractors, consumers, etc. Public authorities have also made it possible to set up development programs for all: education, health, security, infrastructure, etc. However, this public interventionism does not in any way mean that the capitalist model is being called into question, as long as it does not interfere with its founding principle: economic power is vested in the owners of capital. This amounts to handing over absolute power to the shareholder, whom the managers must serve, guarantee and impose on all employees, which is very far from our much vaunted democratic models. It is a kind of economic dictatorship that does not say its name. And this dictatorship leads to privileging the shareholders, to the detriment of all the other components of society: employees, suppliers, customers, consumers, citizens, environment...

However, a challenge to the hegemony of the shareholder does not mean the abolition of the market economy. Different organizations already exist, such as small one-person businesses, mutualist organizations, users' cooperatives, and production cooperatives (SCOP and SCIC). However, these alternative forms of enterprise remain too marginal to prevent the domination of large capitalist enterprises and the pressures they exert (rationalizations, takeovers, relocations, financialization...). Nevertheless, we should be able to discuss these alternative models calmly, without falling into the easy shortcuts of the "capitalism versus communism" opposition. Especially since the market economy, regulated and cooperative, can prove to be collectively more efficient and equitable than the traditional capitalist model, because it is likely to promote a development that is more respectful of humans and the environment, beyond mere economic growth.

Moreover, we too often evoke the term capitalism by considering it to be immutable and uniform. Yet capitalism has changed since its rise at the end of the 18th century. From an industrial capitalism of workshops, it has evolved into a capitalism of large industries, then of services. Today it has become a financial capitalism, globalized and deregulated, where large transnational oligopolistic groups dominate the entire value chain. Not all capitalisms are comparable; the one we are currently experiencing is surely the worst. Markets are suffocated by a relentless financial logic of short-term profitability, and much less by an industrial logic of investment, development and innovation. The wealth created no longer flows from the top to the bottom. Worse, the mechanism has been reversed. The dominant ones succeed in capturing an increasing part of the wealth produced and divert it from the "real" economy. They do not hesitate to destroy our planet in order to accumulate more and more, like a frantic race to the abyss. What profits are they making on their social and ecological failures? What are the environmental costs of the lifestyle of the rich? And how can we ask the poorest to be more sober when the rich allow themselves luxury villas, yachts, private jets, even tourist flights into space? This reality can only lead us to a mortifying schizophrenia. The capitalist model thus seems far from optimal and even raises the question of its medium-term viability. We should think about it, in order to lay new, more virtuous foundations, even if our conclusions are opposed to the interests of the dominant caste.

20. That's the way it is and there's nothing we can do about it

How can a people accept a system that generates and aggravates social injustices and slowly destroys our planet? The nobility legitimized itself by divine right. Dictatorships resort to fear. As for capitalism, it was able to impose itself by law, a law concocted by the bourgeoisie, to its advantage. When the bourgeoisie took the reins of power, it was able to write its rules into law, in the name of freedom, for its own benefit. By granting new rights to the people, the big bourgeoisie was able to add laws establishing the power of "proprietorship". These laws have evolved over the last few decades, adjusting to globalization and the financialization of the economy, reinforcing the interests of the economic elite.

What are our means of action today in the face of a globalized system and the omnipotence of finance and multinationals? Especially since this plutocratic regime is supported by the numerous media that a few billionaires own. With this media concentration, France is only ranked 34th in the world in terms of press freedom in 2021, according to Reporters Without Borders, far behind the countries of Northern Europe and after several countries in South America and Africa. How much space is given to substantive debates, how unbiased are they, especially on issues that could reconsider the place of the dominant? We only need to look at the new liberal doxa, which sets up competitiveness as an absolute, the most socially fragile as "lazy" and "assisted", or even as "agitators" or "haters" when they dare to demonstrate, as we have seen during the Yellow Vests crisis. The privileged would thus no longer be the multimillionaire, necessarily deserving, but rather the poor who abuse the welfare state. A shame. The Covid-19 health crisis shook these fine speeches for a while, with the role played by the "first of the chores" coming back to the forefront in these difficult times, but it hardly lasted. The neoliberal propaganda is once again in full swing, supported by a number of editorialists and experts put forward by the dominant caste, in order to justify the enrichment of a minority and the increase in social injustices, and to present them as a lesser evil, as a collateral damage of the global competition that is imposed on everyone (and which no one wanted, of course) and of unpredictable economic and health crises. The objective is to preserve, at all costs, a large support of the people towards its economic elites by the constitution of a large "elite bloc", and thus to circumscribe any opposition, any "contesting bloc", even if this one is only widening, because the people are less and less fooled.

The adherence, at least relative, of the population to the system remains essential to maintain the stability of the regime in place... and therefore of its ruling class. This works all the better because the richest never appear on the front line. The powerful keep a low profile, as in the time of the kings of Assyria or the Medes, who appeared little in public, giving themselves "something superhuman" and "mysterious", in order to be "served all the more willingly" as the people "did not know who their master was, or even if they had one", as La Boétie evokes in Discourse on Voluntary Servitude. They leave room for their henchmen: experts and editorialists chosen for their political line, heads of foundations that they finance, senior civil servants to whom they offer good opportunities in the private sector...

So, how to fight? Numerous alternative approaches are flourishing locally: sustainable development, healthy food and short circuits, a return to crafts and a certain simplicity of life, respect for nature, solidarity networks, the importance of the commons and cooperation. However, they risk being confined to the margins in the face of a financial capitalism that has imposed itself everywhere. All local actions are useful, but they cannot really constitute real alternatives as long as they are not accompanied by more structural changes. Of course, systemic change is always difficult to achieve because it involves changing at least one of the pillars of the model. How can this be done? Only the constitution of a "protest bloc", united around common proposals for progress, and with a majority in the face of the "elite bloc", could prove convincing. Although protests are multiplying, they are unable to unite. It is true that everything is done by the dominant to divide people by finding multiple scapegoats for our misfortunes: the unemployed, the foreigner, the precarious, the trade unionist, the civil servant, the old man, the Muslim, the leftist, the rural, the suburbanite, the car driver, the non-vaccinated, etc. We must therefore find a clear line of proposals capable of creating a broad adhesion of the "people-class", in order to profoundly change the system, while preserving what works. A better redistribution of wealth will be one of the conditions of success, in order to find a social cohesion... which is currently cracking on all sides.

Conclusion: Proposals on the right to wealth

There are three categories of proposals: those that help reduce the drawbacks of a system, those that transform the system to remove the sources of the problems, and a complete system change.

The first category includes the most numerous proposals: raising taxes on the rich, providing financial assistance to the poorest, legislating protection for the most vulnerable, providing accessible public services, etc. Western countries have already implemented many measures in this direction, without solving the basic problem of inequality; and the globalization of the economy has further reduced the effectiveness of all corrective measures. The "social gains" are being undermined and misused... to the point where they are sometimes purely and simply called into question. Corrective measures remain essential, but they are not sufficient to reverse the systemic trend of wealth concentration in a globalized financial capitalism. Proposals on the evolution of corporate governance and the status of companies also appear to be an interesting way forward, by developing associative, mutualist and cooperative models. But here again, they will probably not be enough to avoid the domination of multinationals. Countering the domination of the economic elite seems increasingly difficult.

The second category of proposals is little mentioned. Any measure of this type is taken with great circumspection, even fear, and must face the systematic opposition of the dominant class. It is not a question here of changing the model, but of questioning at least one of the foundations of this model, likely to modify the balance of power between the dominant and the dominated. There are many ways of doing this, but the technical difficulties of implementing them and the risks of destructuring the whole model reduce their feasibility. While working on the subject, I nevertheless discovered that it would be technically feasible to modify one of the pillars of capitalism, without jeopardizing the whole system: capping incomes and wealth. This proposal is not new. It has already been mentioned by Plato, Robespierre and Proudhon. I am fully aware of the changes that this cap implies. It will impact both the dominant position of the economic elite and our reference points. However, I remain convinced that if the pure and simple suppression of private property, as advocated by some communists, is an extreme position, the right to unlimited wealth is just as extreme.

The ceiling on income and wealth in no way calls into question the right to private property. It simply circumscribes it to a level that would be considered largely satisfactory to one's own needs. Today, the concentration of wealth generates positions of domination that unbalance human relations and the freedom of economic inclusion of each individual. However, this ceiling would only concern the top one percent of the richest population, or even less, depending on the thresholds chosen. With 1% of the French population earning *a minimum of* €10,000 per month and owning €2 million net of debts, we could consider these amounts as a basis for reflection to determine the thresholds we would like to see.

This measure has the advantage of technical simplicity for its implementation, via a tax on income and wealth. The income tax would rise to a marginal rate of 100% above a certain income and the wealth tax would reach 100% above a certain value of wealth. When such a measure is applied, the wealthiest would have to part with some of their wealth. Since a large part of the wealth of the rich is not liquid, it would be a matter of transferring property and not paying a tax. It would then be appropriate to create a public agency dedicated to investment, like a sovereign wealth fund that would recover these properties: company shares, real estate, financial investments. Thanks to the rents of this capital and possible transfers (housing to first-time buyers, company shares to employees...), this agency could undertake a real investment policy, for an ecological transition and quality public services. I estimate the investment capacity of such a sovereign fund at 150 billion euros per year. This is enormous and sufficient to offer us new perspectives in the face of our many challenges. While this may seem like a radical measure, I can't think of any other measure that would provide us with such investment capacity. How can we succeed if we do not commit sufficient resources? This agency could also play a more virtuous shareholder role in all the companies it owns in a non-marginal way, prioritizing hiring and investment over short-term profitability.

To be effective, this measure should obviously not be applied according to place of residence, as is currently the case for income tax and wealth tax, otherwise all the rich will certainly go into exile. This measure should be applied on the basis of nationality in order to not only avoid tax exile, but better still, to put an end to it. Nationality as a reference to a tax is perfectly feasible and is already applied in many countries and in different areas. It should be noted that the acquisition of a new nationality would not prevent the application of this measure. Indeed, it would then be necessary to renounce one's original nationality. However, renouncing French nationality is prohibited for tax reasons and could therefore, in such a case, be refused, at least temporarily, while this measure is applied. And since the tax authorities know the assets of the richest people (except those hidden in tax havens), they would not have the possibility to evade the law by expatriating or opting for a new nationality. This measure would thus be applicable in a single country, without requiring the adhesion of many countries to succeed.

Obviously, the richest people are likely to oppose such a measure with force. If this measure is technically easy to implement, it is politically much more difficult to impose, I am aware of that. Yet it would affect no more than 1% of the population, or 500,000 adults. Why should we reduce the rights of the unemployed or pensioners, who number in the millions, and not those of the richest? We must realize that the right to wealth is only a political right granted to the richest, whereas it is neither economically nor socially necessary. The rich will be able to continue to live very well and to run companies if they wish, but without reaping the fruits of this alone, and without deciding alone. They will still be able to earn comfortable incomes and benefit from a much higher wealth than the "average" French person. This measure is actually not that radical.

Of course, a change in our Constitution would be necessary to apply such a measure. However, it is not a hindrance if a majority of French people approve it. Our French Constitution has already been revised many times since it was established on October 4, 1958, notably during the modernization of the institutions and the construction of Europe. It would suffice, by referendum vote, to modify article 17 of our Constitution by writing that "property being an inviolable and sacred right, no one can be deprived of it, except when public necessity, legally ascertained, obviously requires it, and under the condition of a fair and prior compensation up to a limit to be defined in the law". Moreover, France has already confiscated property without compensation: from the nobles in 1792, or more recently during the nationalization of the Renault company in 1945, which had collaborated with the German occupier. Moreover, public necessity is justifiable in a situation of environmental and social crisis.

Do we dare to attack the privileges of the rich? I am convinced that if we do not tackle head-on the excesses of the market economy, we will only perpetuate a model of oligarchic domination, that of the rich, whatever else we do. If we don't make a break, we will never find sufficient means to take up the multiple challenges that face us: to promote social ascension, to succeed in the ecological transition, to reinvest in our country, to reinforce the financing of our pensions and health expenses, etc. Otherwise, let's be sure that efforts will be asked from the citizens every time, on unemployment, pensions, travel, debt, salaries, by explaining to them that it is normal that the "average" Frenchmen tighten their belts, and never the richest. Should we accept this?

Let us be sure that this change would give new perspectives to the 99% of people who were not born rich, in order to found a more equitable, more democratic, more humane society, giving everyone effective dignity, with real means to guarantee it, and not just rights in principle. Such a measure would facilitate, for a large majority of the population, access to the acquisition of housing, to loans, to employee shareholding, to the co-creation of companies. It would also promote cooperation between economic actors, breaking with the logic of endless personal enrichment of a minority. Finally, it would give the public authorities the means to invest colossal sums each year. Our economy would certainly be stimulated, reducing unemployment, social exclusion, poverty and the resulting insecurity, mechanically reducing the need for assistance. However, this proposal does not call into question our entire model. Small owners and entrepreneurs, executives, and all those who save and build up assets would not be affected by such a cap. It is not a question of impoverishing the population, but of better distributing wealth with a view, on the contrary, to boosting the economy and the inclusion of all. This proposal could therefore find broad support, as it would benefit 99% of the population, by making only the rich class, i.e. 1% of the population at most, bear the brunt of the effort. For once, let's dare to ask them to make an effort! I detail this proposal in Abolishing the right to wealth and Towards a fairer society: a manifesto for a ceiling on income and wealth.

While this measure may be questionable, it is less radical than a complete change of our system, where the risks of failure would be much greater. It also seems more responsible than letting a system that leads us to the destruction of social cohesion and the environment continue. Possibilities of change exist, much more than we might think, much more than those evoked by a majority of politicians who never question the domination of our economic elite. It remains for us to unite around priority issues and projects, from which the vast majority will benefit, avoiding to disperse ourselves on secondary subjects which divide, which obviously suits the dominant ones.

Bibliographic references

Reference works

ALBERT Éric, *Partager le pouvoir c'est possible. Reinventing the company*, Albin Michel, 2014.

ALVAREDO Facundo, CHANCEL Lucas, PIKETTY Thomas, SAEZ Emmanuel, ZUCMAN Gabriel (coord.), *Global Inequality Report 2018*, Seuil, 2018.

ASKENAZY Philippe, *Tous rentiers ! Pour une autre répartition des richesses*, Éditions Odile Jacob, 2016.

ATKINSON Anthony B., *Inequality*, Seuil, 2016.

CHAUVEL Louis, *La Spirale du déclassement*, Seuil, 2016.

CORDELLIER Serge (dir.), *La Mondialisation au-delà des mythes*, La Découverte/Poche Essais, 2000.

DEATON Angus, *The Great Escape: Health, wealth and the origin of inequality*, Princeton University Press, 2013

EYSENCK Michael W., *Happiness: Fact and Myths*, Lawrence Erlbaum Associates, 1990.

COPERNIC Foundation, Towards a fairer society: manifesto for a cap on income and wealth, Les liens qui libèrent, 2019.

GADREY Jean, *Farewell to growth: living well in a world of solidarity*, Les Petits matins, 2015.

JORION Paul, *Le Capitalisme à l'agonie*, Fayard, 2011.

JORION Paul, *Misère de la pensée économique*, Fayard, 2012.

LA BOÉTIE, *Discours de la servitude volontaire (Discourse of Voluntary Servitude)*, published by Mille et une nuits, 1576 text translated into modern French by Séverine Auffret, 1995.

LANDAIS Camille, PIKETTY Thomas, SAEZ Emmanuel, *Pour une révolution fiscale*, Seuil, 2011.

LORDON Frédéric, *Capitalisme, désir et servitude*, La fabrique éditions, 2010.

MASLOW Abraham H., *Theory of Human Motivation*, Psychological Review, 1943.

PIFF Paul K., *Higher social class predicts increased unethical behavior*, Proceedings of the National Academy of Sciences (PNAS), 2012.

PIKETTY Thomas, *Le Capital au xxi siècle*, Seuil, 2013.

PIKETTY Thomas, *Capital and Ideology*, Seuil, 2019.

PINçON Michel and PINçON-CHARLOT Monique, *La Violence des riches. Chronicle of an immense social break-up*, Zones, 2013.

RICHARD Philippe, *Abolishing the Right to Fortune*, Couleur livres, 2017.

ROSANVALLON Pierre (dir.), *Refaire société*, Seuil, 2011.

ROSANVALLON Pierre, *The Society of Equals*, Points Essais, 2013.

SCHWARTZ Shalom, "Les valeurs de base de la personne: théorie, mesures et applications," *Revue française de sociologie*, 2006/4 (vol. 47).

STIGLITZ Joseph E., *The Price of Inequality*, Babel Essay, 2014.

SCHUMPETER Joseph, *Capitalism, Socialism and Democracy*, 1943, French translation by Payot, 1951.

ZUCMAN Gabriel, *The Hidden Wealth of Nations. Enquête sur les paradis fiscaux*, La République des idées - Seuil, 2013.

Statistical references

Acoss, the central agency for social security organizations

World Bank

Bank for International Settlements (BIS)

Ceo-Rexecode

Challenges (ranking of the most wealthy French people)

United Nations Conference on Trade and Development (UNCTAD)

Conseil des prélèvements obligatoires

Financial Stability Board (FSB)

Credit Suisse, *Global Wealth Databook*

Crédoc

DARES

Deloitte and Cadremploi, "Quality of life at work: and happiness?",
2015

Directorate for Research, Studies and Statistics (Dares)

Economic Affairs

Eurostat

France Stratégie

International Monetary Fund (IMF)

Forbes (world wealth ranking)

National Institute of Statistics and Economic Studies (INSEE)

Kantar BrandZ brand ranking

Multinationals Observatory (multinationals.org)

International Labour Organization (ILO)Organization for Economic Cooperation and Development (OECD)

World Trade Organization (WTO)

Oxfam

United Nations Development Programme (UNDP)

UNCTADSTAT of UNCTAD

URSSAF

Contents

www.ingramcontent.com/pod-product-compliance
Lightning Source LLC
LaVergne TN
LVHW051200060726
842526LV00014B/3297